Before
You
Think
Another
Thought

BEFORE
YOU
THINK
ANOTHER

THOUGHT

Bruce I. Doyle III

An Illustrated Guide to Understanding How
Your Thoughts and Beliefs Create Your Life

 HAMPTON ROADS
PUBLISHING COMPANY, INC.

Cover design by Jane Hagaman

For information write:

Hampton Roads Publishing Company, Inc.

134 Burgess Lane
Charlottesville, VA 22902
Or call: (804) 296-2772
FAX: (804) 296-5096
e-mail: hrpc@hrpub.com
Web site: http://www.hrpub.com

If you are unable to order this book from your local
bookseller, you may order directly from the publisher.
Quantity discounts for organizations are available.
Call 1-800-766-8009, toll-free.

ISBN 1-57174-076-7

10 9 8 7 6 5 4 3 2 1

Printed on acid-free paper in Canada

To Wholeness—Yours, Mine, and Ours

It was one of those mornings—
a cloud hid the sun,
Looking up, the bear said,
"Oh, this is no fun!"

So she started to think
about fields full of flowers
And bright, shining rainbows
that follow the showers.

Then she smiled a big smile
for she knew suddenly,
A day is as nice
as you think it to be.

Contents

Preface

What I am about to share with you comes straight from the heart. It's about what I have experienced and what is true for me. I offer no scientific proof for any of my comments. Most of my analogies are simple in an attempt to illustrate what—scientifically—must be beyond human comprehension. They are presented only to give you something to which you can relate.

If what I have to say inspires you to want to know more, I have accomplished my mission, to spread the word that we are all unlimited beings and only our individual beliefs hold us back. Our beliefs originate from those thoughts that we have accepted as true. Every one of our thoughts is a thread in the fabric of what we experience as our lives. And each one of us weaves our own cloth. Collectively, we weave the tapestry of Life—which we *all* experience.

If the life you are experiencing isn't fulfilling, my hope is that by understanding the "fundamentals of thought" you will gain new insights into achieving the life you deserve. One that has no limits.

Acknowledgments

Thanks to each individual who has ever played a role in my life. I now know that you were there to reflect back to me my own projections and beliefs about myself. I finally got it. For those of you whom I blamed—please forgive me. To those who inspired me—I bow.

Many thanks to the following reviewers of my initial manuscript for their comments and suggestions: Anne-Marie Bercik, Henrietta Buck, Shirley Calkins Smith, Guido DiGregorio, Stephanie Farrell, Anne Gouzy, Victoria Heasley, John Herman, Ginger Holler, Harry Palmer, Elaine Phillips, John Phillips, Eddy Savary, Harriett Simon Salinger, Betty Souls, and Leon Stuckenschmidt.

Many thanks also to Sydne Heather Schinkel, author of *Earthbridge Crossing*, and to her husband, Thomas, for their excellent editing and professional contribution to the revised edition.

Special thanks to Sharron Barron of Finally Unlimited for providing the "We's" teachings—my introduction to belief systems.

Special thanks also to Harry Palmer for creating the Avatar Course. Avatar gave me a deeper understanding of belief systems and provided me with additional tools for moving closer to experiencing unlimited living.

Deep appreciation to Maureen Farrell for her creative contribution to bringing forth this book.

And finally, heartfelt thanks to the part of me that now has the courage to share things with you—about myself—that a short time ago would have been unthinkable. May my sharing be helpful.

Love and appreciation to all.

Introduction

Have you ever had the feeling that you were like a small canoe floating in the ocean—solely at the whim of the overpowering waves? No matter how hard you paddled, you could make no impact on your course—you felt totally out of control?

With all the books, tapes, workshops, and seminars available on various aspects of personal development—from basic attitude adjustment to spiritual enlightenment—there still seem to be a great many people on the planet with this out-of-control feeling, trying desperately to gain control over their lives. You may be one of them. Self-esteem for many is at an all-time low. What's going on? What's missing?

What's missing is a clear understanding of the fundamentals of how each of us creates our own life experiences. Yes,

I said *our own*. We are all responsible for our own experiences.

Thoughts and beliefs are the basic elements of all creation. They exist as tiny waves of energy called *thoughtforms*, whose sole purpose is to carry out the intent of the thinker.

By understanding how your thoughts and beliefs operate, you will be able to see how some of the limiting beliefs that you hold keep you from achieving your goals. These beliefs can be removed.

Understanding that you have an *energetic signature* which is derived from your beliefs will help you understand how you attract certain events, circumstances, and relationships into your life. By changing your beliefs you will attract new, more desirable experiences.

When you realize that your thoughts and beliefs determine what you experience, you're on your way to having mastery over your life.

one

How Thoughts Work

Thought

Did you ever have thoughts that you didn't want to share? Thoughts about other people that you knew would upset them if you verbalized them? Maybe about their clothes, manners, or things they did that bothered you. You hesitated to share your thoughts because you wanted to maintain peace in the relationship. You may have even berated yourself for having such awful thoughts—"How could I think such a thing?"

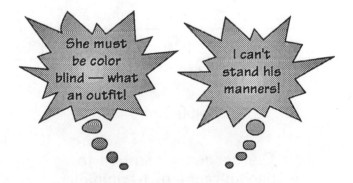

Most people consider thoughts as ideas or notions that reside in their heads for their own private use. Thoughts help you to figure out things, evaluate situations, make decisions, and generate feelings, and sometimes they seem to drive you crazy (well, almost).

Thoughts or ideas may seem to reside in your head but, in reality, each thought exists as a minute wave of energy called a thought-form. A thoughtform is real—it exists. It happens to not be noticed by you because its energy vibration (frequency) is outside the range of human senses. It operates faster than the speed of light and is, therefore, not visible to you.

Energy Spectrum

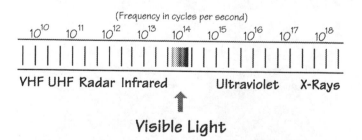

(Frequency in cycles per second)

10^{10} 10^{11} 10^{12} 10^{13} 10^{14} 10^{15} 10^{16} 10^{17} 10^{18}

VHF UHF Radar Infrared   Ultraviolet   X-Rays

Visible Light

Our senses are limited to a specific range of frequencies.

It might be helpful for you to understand this concept by relating it to something you already know but to which you probably have not given much thought. If you're like most of us, you have a favorite radio station. Perhaps an FM station for listening to "your kind" of music. Let's say it's 102.7 on the dial.

What that number means is that the frequency of transmission for that station is 102.7 megahertz (megacycles). *Mega* is the metric designation for one million. The energy transmitted by the station vibrates continuously in the space around you. But, unless your radio is tuned to the frequency of 102.7 million cycles per second, you are unaware of it.

My point is this: There is a lot of information vibrating in the space around us that we are not aware of because our senses are limited to a specific range of frequencies. And some of the information vibrating in the space is in the form of tiny, subtle thoughtforms.

The mission of each thoughtform is to fulfill the intent of the thought—to carry out the thinker's desires or intentions. It does so by attracting to it similar thoughtforms to help it fulfill itself. In effect, you are like a radio station, WYOU, broadcasting your desires, intentions, and ideas out into the universe—completely uncensored. Picture a king who sends se-lected members of his court out into his king-dom to fulfill his desires (even his secret ones).

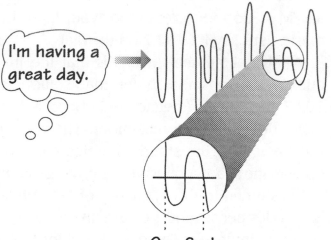

I'm having a great day.

One Cycle

Thoughts exist as thoughtforms

Have you ever had someone say to you, "Watch what you wish for; you're liable to get it"? Have you ever had the same thought, at exactly the same time, as someone close to you? Have people ever accused you of read-ing their minds? Are there people in your life that you feel "tuned-in" to? Some individuals are very sensitive to picking up thoughtform vibrations. If you answered *yes* to any of these questions, you are probably one of them.

Beliefs

Thoughts that you accept as true become your beliefs.

Together, all of your individual beliefs make up your belief system.

If I told you that the moon is made of Swiss cheese, I doubt that you would believe me. Based on what you already know, you wouldn't consider it to be true and it would not become part of your belief system. But if I said, "The weather patterns around the world are going to continue to change dramatically," you would probably agree. Some of you have real tangible evidence of this already. You would feel that my statement is true and add it to your already-existing beliefs.

Beliefs are specialized thoughtforms that become part of your individual belief system. Furthermore, existing as waves of energy that you radiate out into the universe, they accumulate similar thoughtforms in order to create events, circumstances, and relationships that substantiate your beliefs.

"Wait a minute," you say. "Don't you have that backwards? I experience something—then I can believe it. You know the old saying, 'I'll believe it when I see it.'"

Yes, that is a very old saying, but in reality it happens the other way around. You will experience something only if you believe it. The belief must come first. If you experienced something that you didn't believe, how could you believe it? Your experience confirms your belief—belief precedes experience. It's the way the universe works.

Belief precedes experience.

If you believe that you're poor, can you experience being rich? If you believe that you're fat, can you experience being thin? If you believe that you're dumb, can you experience being smart? Think about it! What you believe is what you experience.

Beliefs are usually described as either conscious beliefs or subconscious beliefs.

Conscious beliefs are those that you are aware of; with some prompting you could write down a few. Conscious beliefs can be empowering—such as "I'm smart" and "Life's exciting"—or limiting—such as "I'm clumsy" and "Men hate me."

Subconscious beliefs are beliefs that you are not aware of. You are unaware that they exist, and the experiences they create for you are seen as "That's the way life is." You have no sense of responsibility for having accepted them as beliefs. The beliefs are transparent to you.

An example of a limiting subconscious belief might be "I can never have things my way," stemming from a childhood decision about authority. This belief could show up as repeated conflicts with bosses later in life. Such a person might frequently state, "All bosses are jerks," not realizing that he is operating out of a transparent belief. As you know, not all people experience their bosses that way.

An example of an empowering subconscious belief might be something like "I'm always safe." People with this belief might not be aware of it, yet live their lives out of having no fear for their safety. They would simply not attract a potentially harmful situation and would see no threat to themselves even if one arose.

BELIEFS

	EMPOWERING	LIMITING
CONSCIOUS	• I'm smart • Things work out for me • I'm healthy • Life's exciting	• I'm not very smart • I can't . . . . • I'll always be fat • I'm clumsy • Men hate me
SUBCONSCIOUS	• The world is safe • I'll be taken care of • I belong • I'm OK	• I'm a failure • Nobody loves me • I don't deserve happiness • The world is scary

(MIND)

In my belief model you can see that there are basically four areas of beliefs that can be considered. At the conscious and the subconscious levels you have both empowering and limiting beliefs. It's the limiting beliefs that we'll discuss in more detail. After you eliminate these beliefs, you will expend less energy and attention creating the circumstances that you choose to have in your life.

Every thought and every belief has its corresponding thoughtform which is a dynamic wave of energy that has two key parameters: a *frequency of vibration* corresponding to its intent and a *magnitude* corresponding to the amount of desire associated with it. Each of our belief systems can be represented by an energetic signature (not unlike our personalized signature) which is unique to us and essentially defines us. We are all like energetic magnets drawing our experiences to us.

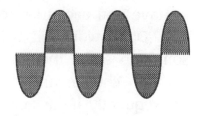

Amount of Desire
(Magnitude)

Intent
(Frequency)
in Cycles per Second

**Every thoughtform has
two key parameters.**

Have you ever noticed that, when you meet them for the first time, you feel comfortable with some people and you don't feel comfortable with others? You're sensing their energy fields. The ones with whom you feel comfortable will most likely have similar beliefs. Trust your feelings.

When you are in close relationships with people, you can feel that they are upset before they say a word. You can sense that their energy has shifted—to a lower frequency.

Your basic energy signature is the sum of all your thoughts and beliefs. You define yourself—personality, physical attributes, and behavior. You are the only one who can create or change your thoughts and your beliefs. And your beliefs create what you experience as life.

Have you ever tried to change someone else? Didn't work, did it? No one can change someone else's thoughts. Individuals must want to change and do so on their own. Consequently, if each of us is responsible for our own thoughts, we are likewise responsible for our own feelings. Your feelings are generated by your thoughts. Notice that when you have positive thoughts, you feel good. When you think negative thoughts, how do you feel?

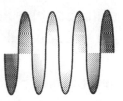

**Your energetic signature
attracts your life's circumstances.**

Have you ever been accused of hurting others' feelings? When you realize that you can't create their thoughts, you likewise understand that you can't create their feelings. How freeing! Now you can let go of the old belief that we all grew up with: "You shouldn't hurt other people's feelings." Naturally, there is appropriateness in all things. But you can't determine others' feelings—their feelings are strictly theirs.

My daughter Megan's college psychology text has an example of a man who is severely bumped from behind on a crowded subway. His immediate reaction is raw anger—the source of which is his visualization of a large robust women bullying her way through the crowd. As he turns to confront her, he realizes that the person who bumped him is blind. His feelings immediately shift as his mind fills with thoughts of compassion. His thoughts—his feelings.

Do you remember your experience—how you felt—when you believed in Santa Claus? Quite exciting, wasn't it? What was your experience when you found out that he really didn't exist and you changed your belief? Took a lot of fun out of your life, didn't it? Different belief—different experience!

It's true!

When more than one person agrees on something, it becomes a shared belief.

Shared beliefs can extend to many individuals. The different religions operating on the planet are examples of many individuals sharing common beliefs. All the various social, financial, and political structures around the globe are also examples of belief systems. The important thing to remember is that each individual has the right to his or her own experiences, and consequently to his or her own beliefs.

Everyone has his own truth.

It's when you try to convince others that your beliefs are the *only* truth, that difficulty arises. You see, we all have our own truths. Truth belongs to the believer. There are as many truths as there are believers. Many can share common beliefs, but essentially each of us creates our own unique perspective of the world based on our beliefs.

In essence then, each of us lives in and is responsible for our own world. Certainly your world is different than mine and likewise that of your neighbors. Did you ever wonder how you appear to someone else? Did you ever wonder what it was like to walk in someone else's shoes? We all see life from our own perspectives (based on our beliefs), and for each person it's different. In fact, the only real difference in any of us is what we believe. Sure, many of us look different, but maybe that's also a belief.

If you find yourself trying to convince someone about something you believe, ask yourself if you really believe it. Needing to convince someone else about your truth would imply that you doubt your own belief. When you really believe something, there is no doubt. *Hoping* it might be true would allow for doubt. When you have no doubt, you can stand in the face of any challenge unshaken and without emotion—you know the truth.

Thoughtform Structure

Understanding the structure of thought-forms will greatly assist you in understanding their impact on belief systems.

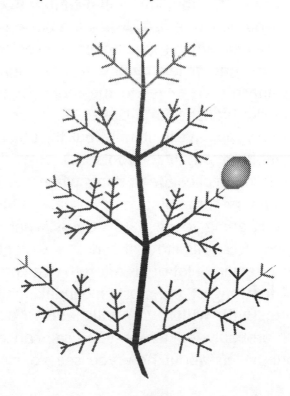

In my view, thoughtforms tend to cluster and aggregate, much as a clump of grapes. Take a clump of grapes, pull off the grapes, and you have an array of branches going off in all directions. As you go back toward the main branch, the branches get thicker and stronger. You end up with the "core" branch.

In my analogy, the core branch equates to the "root" thoughtform—the initial and deep-rooted thoughtform that is the primary cause of the issue involved. With any new idea, issue, or situation, the initial thoughtform that you generate establishes the basic pattern or blueprint of experience. Subsequent thoughts and beliefs relating to that subject will attach themselves to the root thoughtform like branches in a cluster. To clear out an issue, you have to literally "pull the original thoughtform out by the roots."

A former colleague of mine, whenever he encounters something new, usually states, "This is going to be hard." Guess what he experiences? His life is a series of struggles which require a lot of his effort to overcome.

The strongest and most influential limiting beliefs with which you will have to deal will probably be about your self-concept (your beliefs about how you see yourself).

Your *"I am _____"* statements. These beliefs usually originate in infancy and/or childhood. They are often referred to as "conditioning" or "programming."

I will not use either of these terms. To me, they imply that something was done "to you," tending to generate blame and avoid self-responsibility. No one other than the believer—you—can accept or choose a belief.

So, even as an infant you did the choosing. Since the experience probably involved a caretaker or someone in an influential position, you naturally accepted that person's assessment. What reason did you have to doubt their assessment of you? None.

But now, as an adult, you can re-evaluate your decision, to see if you still wish to hold specific beliefs that are no longer in your best interest. Beliefs are like ideas—good ones you keep, bad ones you discard.

An Empowering Example

Let's look at the favorable impact of an empowering belief first.

Jane, as a small child, had a very positive environment. She was loved by her parents, siblings, and friends. She was encouraged to try things and was given praise and supported. She adopted the belief, "I always have everything I need and I am secure."

Jane's Thoughtform Structure

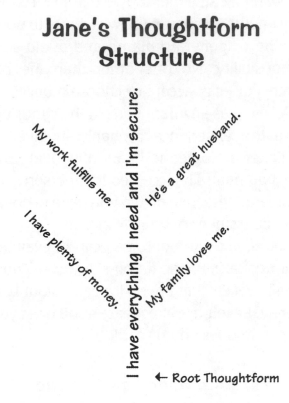

My work fulfills me.

I have everything I need and I'm secure.

He's a great husband.

I have plenty of money.

My family loves me.

← Root Thoughtform

That basic belief, in order to fulfill itself, acted to positively influence every major facet of her life. Throughout her life, unless impacted by a conflicting belief, she experienced that belief. As an adult, she saw its effect in her work—a fulfilling job. Her finances continually sustained her needs. Her relationships were satisfying and stable and provided her with the love that she deserved. That strong empowering belief provided a very supportive "root" for her life's experiences.

A Limiting Example

Jim, on the other hand, was not as fortunate. Jim's environment stemmed from a marriage that was not planned. His father married his mother because he thought doing so was his duty; but he was extremely resentful of Jim for having been born. He paid little attention to Jim except to criticize or severely discipline him. Fortunately, Jim's mother was caring and loved him dearly. But her affection for him only angered his jealous father.

Out of all of this, Jim soon decided (created the belief) that it was his fault that his parents were unhappy. This translated into, "I'm responsible for others' unhappiness." Can you see how that "root" belief would negatively impact every major area of Jim's life? What a burden to feel responsible for other people's unhappiness—a life of trying to please others.

How would Jim, as an adult, negotiate a deal or ask for a raise if he thought the other person might get upset? Can you imagine Jim trying to please his mate all of the time? How would it feel to Jim if someone around him wasn't happy? He would always feel like it was his fault. A life for Jim of no emotional freedom for himself—always monitoring his behavior. That's what a limiting belief does. And to Jim, his behavior felt normal—the limitation was transparent to him.

Jim's Thoughtform Stucture

I hate this job.

She'll leave if I say no.

I can't ask for money.

I'm responsible for other's unhappiness.

I need permission.

← Root Thoughtform

Again, remember that there is no blame for Jim's father—it was Jim who decided to accept what he believed about himself. At the time, it may have made a lot of sense. A very strong limiting factor in the blueprint for determining Jim's life experience was put in place by what might appear to be a simple, harmless belief.

Life Incidents

Once a root thoughtform is established, incidents will occur to continue to provide evidence to the believer that the belief is true. Let's try another example to further illustrate the point.

Sally's mother had to attend an unexpected business meeting during a time when her regular sitter was not available. After several phone calls, her mother was finally able to reach a neighbor who agreed to look after the child. The neighbor was a nice lady, but she was not used to being around four-year-old children.

Sally sensed her awkwardness. She didn't feel at all comfortable with the new sitter and started to cry. The sitter, trying to get her to stop, began a series of make-believe games that involved making strange faces. This just added to Sally's fear and she cried harder. The sitter, in sheer frustration, picked up Sally, took her into her bedroom and flopped her on the bed. As the sitter slammed the door behind her, she hollered, "You're the worst kid I've ever seen." Sally, in that moment of vulnerability, decided, "There's something wrong with me."

Sally's Life

Age 4	Age 6	Age 16	Age 30	Age 40
Root	Poor	Poor	Missed	Divorced
Incident	Eyes	Grades	Promotions	

As Sally grew older, incidents occurred and similar thoughtforms were created to fulfill the intent of the core belief, "There's something wrong with me." These similar thoughtforms attached to the root thoughtform like the branches of the grapevine cluster we've discussed. All areas of her life became affected by this very basic core belief—of which, by the way, she was totally unaware.

Sally's Thoughtform Structure

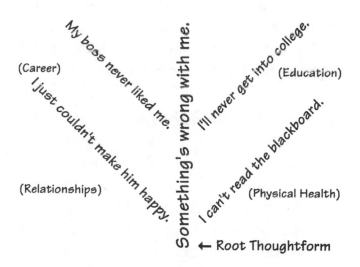

The figure on the preceding page contains some examples of real-life situations that could stem from an early belief that "there is something wrong with me." The related beliefs about poor eyesight at six years of age, difficulty with academics in the teens, work issues at age thirty, and a relationship issue at age forty could all develop from the one, simple, limiting belief, "There's something wrong with me." Naturally, these same situations could be generated from other belief sources. If you relate to one of these conditions, don't assume it's the same belief. Do some exploring: Can you see repeated patterns of experience in the lives of those close to you? What about yourself? Do you keep having a recurring experience? What belief might be behind these situations?

Self-Sabotage

Frequently, people experience unexplained behavior that some would describe as "self-sabotage." It's like having in your subconscious mind a little gremlin who is very mischievous. Every once in a while he does something odd—usually at an inappropriate time—over which you seem to have no control. At least that's the way it appears. It's that misplaced comment during an important meeting that just kills the opportunity you were counting on. You walk out of the meeting muttering to yourself, "Why in the world did I say that?"

Maybe that little gremlin doesn't exist. Consider the existence of a limiting thoughtform for which you are totally responsible—but of which you are not aware. What do you think might happen to someone in an interview who believed, "I just don't do well in interviews"? That person would probably say something unintended at the most inappropriate time. It might be called self-sabotage, but, more than likely, there is a limiting belief at work.

What I'm talking about seems subtle, but can you see the significant impact that these limiting beliefs have on your life? Here's a real-life example.

About a year ago, I was working with a client—I'll call him Pete—who was conducting a nationwide job search. We spent many hours together, mostly with me just listening and observing his frustration. Pete was having a difficult time making a decision about what he wanted to do. It seemed that every day he was excited about something new and was off in a different direction.

I had introduced my concepts about belief systems to Pete and he had an intellectual understanding of what I was saying, but no real, major "a-ha" yet. As Pete and I worked more closely together, I began to make notes of the limiting beliefs that I frequently heard him say. The beliefs I heard most often were:

"There is a price to pay for everything."
"It's not possible to have it all."
"Nothing is what people perceive it to be."

Pete and I discussed these frequently expressed beliefs and it was clear that even though he had an intellectual idea of the concept "Beliefs determine experience," he hadn't internalized it. He was totally unaware that these beliefs were operating. He was so used to his mode of operation that it had become transparent to him.

Once we discussed these limiting beliefs openly, he was able to get in touch with them. He had grown up with them—they were the same as his father's.

Can you see how someone operating with these beliefs would have a difficult time making a decision? He was setting himself up. There was only one right decision for him to make, and he had better make the right choice or he would have hell to pay.

A few days after our discussion, Pete came into my office to tell me that he had shared his new insight with his realtor. He was relating his belief to her that "things aren't what they seem," when she replied, "You're right! All my clients have hidden agendas." Without hesitation, Pete declared, ". . . and she has been a realtor for ten years!"

Pete was still looking for evidence to prove that his belief was true—for everyone.

After I pointed out that his friend was merely attracting the clients who would substantiate her belief, he began to see my point. He was becoming more aware and could begin the process of sorting out those beliefs that were getting in his way.

Attention

What you put your attention on strengthens or expands in your life.

Scientists are discovering more and more evidence that we humans are not independent observers of a mechanical universe. Our attention, backed by the intent of our beliefs, creates what we experience as our lives. Scientifically, one might say that focusing your attention on the energy field of consciousness, which contains the waves of all possibilities, creates the particles (events and materializations) that you experience as your reality.

This is a very important concept. Let me repeat it: What you put your attention on strengthens or expands in your life. This one idea alone can make a big difference for you.

Remember the last time you were considering buying a new car. You had your attention focused on it and what happened? All of a sudden, you noticed many different types, models, and colors of cars, "For Sale" signs in windows, ads in the paper, and people relaying information to you about a friend who was thinking of selling his car. Your attention brought things into your awareness because of your focus. The moment you purchased your new car, your attention shifted. The same information about cars was available, but it was no longer attracted to your awareness. Your attention was focused elsewhere.

What you focus on expands in your life.

Imagine a coal miner with a helmet that contains a light to enable him to see directly in front of him. Now, picture yourself with a similar light beaming from your forehead. Think of it as your attention beam. How often are you aware of where it's focused?

It is important to focus your attention effectively. In other words, don't waste your creative energy. Without deliberate focus, you're spreading your attention around randomly, achieving no real benefit for yourself. Keep your attention focused on something positive, and good things begin to happen.

This is the real reason for goal setting. It's the mental focus that helps you achieve your goals. Your focus is actually strengthening the thoughtform that you have expressed as your goal. Unfortunately, many of us have been oriented to the pass-fail aspect of goal setting and so, to avoid failure, we don't set goals. Yes, the concept of pass-fail is a belief—a very strong shared one.

If there is something in your life that you want, keep your attention focused on that goal. If things show up—and they will—that seem to get in the way, don't focus on them. Handle them, but stay focused on your goal. It's when you focus on the obstacles that you tend to give up. Think about what we have already discussed. What happens when you focus on the obstacles? Right—your focus just strengthens the thoughtforms related to the obstacle. Stay focused on the goal.

You might have a goal that you believe can be achieved only if you have a certain amount of money. Instead of focusing on the goal, you focus on the fact that you don't have enough money. What gets strengthened is the thoughtform for not having enough money. Maybe there was a way to achieve the goal without money. By not focusing on the goal, you restrict possibilities, of which you may not be aware, from occurring.

Victoria Heasley, a massage therapist, constantly amazes me with how she obtains what she needs. She is the kind of person who says to herself, "I sure could use another couch," and within days a friend who is moving out of town calls her to ask if she knows anyone who could use a good couch. If she focused on worrying about the money to buy a couch, she would miss these opportunities. Stay focused on your goal!

Remember the story about the little steam engine who believed he could make it up the mountain. He was really focused on his goal.

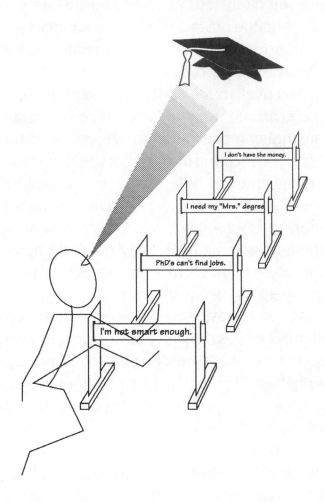

Keep focused on your goal.

How well do you think he would have done chanting, "I'll never make it. My joints are sore. I'll never make it. My joints are sore."?

Knowing where your attention is focused is also important because you physically experience what you focus your attention on. You're probably focused on limiting or negative thoughts any time you are experiencing something unpleasant. So, if you want to change how you feel, shift your attention to something else, anything—a pleasant memory, a different subject. Or, best of all, become an observer of your thoughts and just watch them float by. This can be quite relaxing and can be referred to as meditating. By monitoring where you are focusing your attention, you will begin to gain insight into why you are experiencing what you are experiencing.

As you read through this book, notice your emotions. If you detect uncomfortable ones, see if you can determine what belief you might hold that is being challenged by what you're reading at that moment. Fear, worry, and doubt are probably the three strongest thoughtforms on the planet. They will rob you of all your desires. If you can get in touch with and remove the limiting beliefs behind these culprits, you'll be a new person.

———— two ————

What You Believe
Is What You Get

Self-Responsibility

The fact that you create all your life experiences is a rude awakening for most people.
You may be sitting there right now doubting
every word that I'm saying. And that's OK. All
I ask is that you consider what's being said.
Give It some thought. Be open to the possibil-
ity that it's worth exploring.

The good news is that with the recognition
that you are creating your life (and some
forgiveness thrown in), you can start taking
charge—as the designer of your life, no longer
a victim of life's random circumstances. You
become self-responsible.

Knowing you are responsible for your experiences, and always have been, gives you
the opportunity to start creating the experiences you would like to have, rather than
experiencing life by default. A great deal of
personal power is available to you. Much

more than you've imagined. By personal power, I'm not talking about the kind of power that you have over others. I'm talking about inner power. The power of self-confidence and self-esteem. When you have that kind of power, there is no need or desire to have power over anyone or anything else.

I sometimes reflect on my earlier years as a young manager in the corporate world. A few of our senior executives appeared, to me, to need power—the power-over-others type. It seemed that they wasted a lot of time and talent (theirs) in business review sessions intimidating our management team. They were good at generating fear and stimulating feelings of inadequacy. It's a shame some of them didn't have the personal power to act more like coaches. I'm sure that my peers, and the business, and I would have been better off.

It's nice to look back and see the situation from a new perspective. It feels good to know that their beliefs created their experiences, and my beliefs created mine. This takes away all the blame. What else would some young manager attract to himself if he had the subconscious limiting belief, "It's always my fault"? I was constantly putting myself in situations where I had to defend myself, trying to prove that it wasn't my fault. Not a comfortable position to be in. But that's how limiting thoughtforms work. I'm sure glad that this one has been resolved. As you begin to experience the power of changing your beliefs, your desire to know more and more about it becomes compelling.

The Mirror

When we examine a little further the concept that your beliefs determine your experiences, we will see that your experiences (external events) are driven by your beliefs (internal events). You can then use the outer events to see what you really believe. This is often referred to as *mirroring*.

The universe *you* experience mirrors your belief system back to you. If you want to change your experiences, you must change your beliefs. Your life experiences are great teachers, but if you don't realize that you're in class, you may miss the entire course. Sure, it will be offered again, but you know what happens to tuition every year!

As you work your way through the ideas in this book, it would be helpful if you start making a list of the situations, circumstances, or people that give you unpleasant feelings,

The universe mirrors your beliefs.

as they come to mind. These notes will give you a starting point as you explore later what your mirror has in store for you. Also, consider someone you know very well and jot down what that person might believe, to be having the experiences he or she is having. What about you? Are there some experiences in your life that you would prefer not to have? What beliefs might you hold that are creating these experiences?

In most cases, the reflections of unpleasantness that are mirrored back to you (your perceptions) have to do with beliefs you hold about yourself. Poor self-esteem is the major cause of individuals' dissatisfaction with their lives. The defined inadequacies and limiting beliefs (many of which are transparent) are experienced by seeing in others what we are not seeing, or refuse to accept, about ourselves. Next time you feel critical of someone, reflect back and see if you aren't, in some way, identifying with a trait in yourself that you don't like or haven't accepted.

If you issue a judgment—either verbally or mentally—about someone else's behavior and it's accompanied by emotion, you're getting "hooked." The emotion is a great indicator that you have an opportunity for some self-discovery and possible healing on the issue in question. If you only observe someone else's behavior, just *notice* them without any emotional response, you are clear.

Don't be alarmed if you find yourself issuing judgments. This behavior is something that may take some time to change, should you choose to do so. Every one of those judgments is tied to a belief. It may take a while to track them all down. Be kind to yourself as you do so. Judging yourself for judging others just compounds the issue.

I can recall often hearing, as I was growing up, my grandfather and my dad speak critically and very judgmentally of other people—those who were different from them. Those of another race and people who were poor were deemed "naturally lazy" and those who were "the filthy rich" were "crooks." I didn't think that much of those opinions rubbed off; we had only one black person in school and I liked him a lot. He was always in a good mood and usually had us in stitches. Later in life I had other friends who were different from me.

I never thought, therefore, that I had an issue with race until I fell in love, head over heels, with the woman of my dreams. Shortly after we began dating, she informed me that her previous relationship had been with a black man. I was stunned. My judgment was put right in my face. It wasn't transparent any longer. I had a long list of judgmental beliefs about the kind of white women who would date a black man. I had to either walk away from the relationship to prove that I was right or look at my limiting beliefs. They sure didn't fit my current beliefs about the woman I was dating. The mental conflict was agonizing.

Fortunately, she was understanding and I was able to get in touch with my limiting beliefs about the situation and release them. It took several tough months of soul-searching to let go of them—not to mention the male insecurity issues it dug up.

Judgments are tied to beliefs.

Things always happen for a good reason. Several years later, my youngest daughter introduced us to her new boyfriend during parents' weekend at college. You guessed it—he was black. I was pleased that it didn't bother me a bit. He was a nice young man. It felt good to have that issue behind me, too.

Each time you let go of a limiting belief, life gets calmer and calmer. The mental chatter just diminishes. It's your assessment (perception) of external events that creates your experience of them. If you don't like what you're experiencing, you can always revise your assessment of what's happening.

Positive Attitude

With your new understanding of energetic vibrations, thoughtforms, and focus of attention, you should see clearly now why so much emphasis is placed on having a positive attitude—positive beliefs. Positive beliefs create positive thoughtforms, which attract positive events and circumstances into your life.

I used to think having a positive attitude was something that each of us "should" have to be more acceptable. That may be true, but the real impact of being positive has to do with your state of being—your vibrational state—and what it will attract to you.

People who just pretend to have a positive attitude may be more acceptable, but they will still attract according to how they are really vibrating—the energy they are emanating will attract their circumstances. So the message is clear. With your new insight into the fundamentals of thought, you'll want to start immediately making sure you're focused on being positive. Adopt the attitude that everything that happens in your life happens for a good reason. This will get you off to a great start.

In 1978 during a business trip to Chicago, I was snowed in for three days in O'Hare International Airport. There were several feet of snow on the ground and everything was at a standstill. During the second day, the restaurants began running out of food, stranded mothers were overwhelmed with crying children, and people were fed up with the whole situation, mostly from not knowing when it would end.

The range of attitudes that the situation evoked in people was amazing. I saw the worst and I saw the best. Some travelers were downright nasty, greedy, and could think of nothing but themselves. I wondered what they must have been believing about their personal situations to be having such dreadful experiences. On the other hand, most of the people went out of their way to help others, especially those who had small children.

People's experiences of that situation were directly related to what they believed was happening. Next time you're involved in a trying situation, look around and see if you can think of what others might be believing to be having the experiences they are having. It's also revealing to include your own experience. What beliefs might be creating your experience?

I learned a lot from my friend Maureen about positive attitude. She is primarily responsible for my starting to believe that "everything happens for a good reason." Her version is, "Everything happens for the best." I initially began adopting this attitude on faith, but, as I learned more about thoughtforms and energetic attraction, I could see its validity. It keeps you in a positive frame of mind, no matter what happens, so you can continue to emit positive energy and attract positive circumstances. Here's another true story.

For many years, I had been fortunate never to have had a flat tire or a breakdown on the highway. Such inconveniences always occurred where they could be easily handled. That changed about six months ago. I was on my way home from the office when the clutch in my sports car failed as I was pulling away from a stoplight. Luckily, no one was immediately behind me. My first thought was, "I wonder what the benefit of this is going to be."

After pushing the car to the side of the road, I walked across the street and called my auto club emergency number. Within thirty minutes the car was loaded on a flatbed truck and we were on our way. The driver dropped me off at my house and delivered the car to the Porsche garage, Team Stuttgart. I was amazed at how smoothly everything went.

The next day Dusty, my mechanic, called to tell me that a clip had come loose on the clutch cable—a very minor problem. He asked if I was still interested in selling the car. I said that I was. He then informed me that while my car was in the shop, a gentlemen had come in looking for advice on where to buy a good used Porsche. The gentleman liked my

912E, and Dusty hoped that it was OK to have given him my phone number. I sold the car to that same gentleman a week later. Did my clutch cable break for a good reason? I guess it depends on what you believe.

Speaking of attitude, how would you describe your attitude about yourself? Is it positive? Yeah, I know, you can give me a long list of all the things you believe are wrong with you—your body's not perfect (according to whose standards?), you've done some terrible things (says who?), you're this, you're that. Fine, go ahead and make the list and then, without judgment, just lovingly accept yourself. "Accept" doesn't mean anything but that, accept—no judgments. "This is how I see me. I accept myself. It's OK to be me." Say it: "It's OK to be me." Great, again: "It's OK to be me."

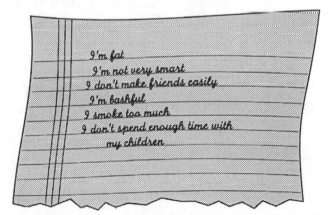

I'm fat
I'm not very smart
I don't make friends easily
I'm bashful
I smoke too much
I don't spend enough time with
    my children

Please note that your list of judgments about yourself (either written or mental) is a list of beliefs. Nothing more—nothing less. They can be changed. Remember—beliefs determine experience. You experience "you" as you have defined yourself. What you believe about yourself must be what you experience; otherwise you wouldn't believe it. Yes, just like circumstances and events, your self-concept is yours—your own beliefs about yourself.

In 1981, I had what many longed for—a good job, a big house, an attractive wife, and three young daughters whom I adored. But at a very deep level, a part of me wanted to be free, and I left a seventeen-year marriage. The guilt over destroying the lives of four people for whom I cared deeply trashed my self-esteem.

During the next six years, the universe reflected back to me my deeply held (transparent) belief that I had done something very bad for which I deserved to be punished. My second marriage and several executive-level jobs ended in disappointment. Naturally, at the time, I had no idea that my beliefs were creating my experiences.

It was excerpts from an essay that my daughter Ellen wrote for application to college that finally gave me a new perspective on the situation.

"My parents divorced the year I turned 13. At the time, I thought it was the greatest tragedy that could ever happen. But four years later, despite the sadness and confusion, it has provided me with some wonderful opportunities and experiences.

"Traveling to visit my father in various locations, I have also had to be responsible for my younger sister. Our relationship has become very close because we have to depend on each other.

"Because of my parents' divorce, I have had to become more independent at an earlier age than I might have otherwise had to do. I think learning to do lots of things myself rather than rely on others has helped me in my personal life and schoolwork."

Ellen Doyle
March 1987

This positive point of view allowed me to start examining my own belief that I had damaged my daughters. I realized that my guilt was my own doing. I needed to see the situation in a new light. Now, thirteen years later, all three girls have finished college and are creating successful lives for themselves.

Your acceptance of yourself, just as you are, is the first step in allowing you to explore the limiting beliefs you have about yourself. Acceptance drops away the resistance to experiencing yourself as you are and helps keep your energy positive. It also frees up wasted energy so it can be used in accessing and changing those beliefs that you would like to change. Notice that I said "the ones you would like to change." You are free to believe what you wish. Change only what you wish to change. After all, it's your experience.

Experiencing

I've used the word *experiencing* a lot. What does experiencing really mean? Experiencing as I am referring to it is simply being in touch with what you are feeling. That's the only way you can truly experience anything—you must feel it! It sounds simple enough, but the fact is that many of us don't allow ourselves to feel—consequently we don't fully experience life.

Have you ever driven down the highway and suddenly realized that the past twenty miles went by without you noticing them? Why? Because you had your attention somewhere else. You missed experiencing (the feelings associated with) the beautiful countryside, the sunshine radiating off the autumn leaves, and the two deer grazing just behind the white picket fence.

There is a difference between having the experience of a thirty-minute commute and fully experiencing the ride home from the office.

It was during a Hakomi Therapy training session a few years ago that I finally realized the difference. In Hakomi Therapy, the focus is on getting your client in touch with what they are physically experiencing (feeling) in the present moment about a previous situation, rather than mentalizing (talking about) it. The term "being mindful" is used to describe the concept.

So, to really experience anything fully, you must be mindful—you must place your attention on how you are feeling. Next time you're riding in the car, see if you can experience the trip a little differently.

Have you ever "tuned someone out" because you didn't want the experience (feeling) of being with or listening to them? Make sure you are not "tuning yourself out" of much of your life.

From time to time, we all try to communicate to others how we feel. Words such as "love," "happy," "joyful," and "excited" are verbal symbols for expressing varying degrees of feeling good. "Bored," "hate," "sorrow," and "mad" are symbols for feeling bad. And what you experience either feels good, or it doesn't. No matter how one arrives at it, success for all of us is finding out what makes us feel good. And the only time to feel anything (experience it) is in the present moment—right *now*. Whoops—that "now" is already gone—gone forever.

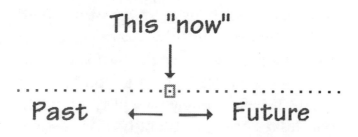

The time line for life is really an infinite line of very short periods of "now—the present moment. Periods of "now" that have already occurred we call history, or the past. We can no longer experience them. That's right! We can no longer experience them.

"But," you say, "I experience a lot of pain about things that happened in the past." That may be true, but you are not experiencing the past; you are experiencing your *beliefs* about the past. This is another one of those subtle distinctions that is quite profound. The same goes for the future. It's your story or beliefs—usually in the form of worry—that will cause unpleasant "nows" to occur. Isn't it amazing how easy it is to keep yourself from enjoying each successive "now—Life!

The importance of being consciously aware of your state during the present "now" has a lot to do with establishing your experience in future "nows." If you are positive in this "now" and are deliberately focused on your desires for the future and you have no limiting beliefs about your ability to create your desires, you can count on your desires manifesting for you. Unfortunately, many of us have doubts about our abilities—just beliefs, but they have a canceling effect on our ability to create. As I mentioned earlier, fear, worry, and doubt are the strongest limiting conditions for most of us.

Mary Burmeister, the Founder of Jin Shin Jyutsu Inc., says, "Worry is prayer for what you do not want" and "Fear is: False Evidence Appearing Real." Also, I heard somewhere that worry is like a rocking chair—it gives you something to do, but it doesn't get you anywhere. When you can remove the limiting beliefs behind fear, worry, and doubt, your life will begin to flow more smoothly.

Why You're Not Getting What You Want

By now it should be clear that what keeps you from realizing your full potential, or your dreams, are the strong limiting beliefs that you hold. Furthermore, the most critical of all your beliefs will have to do with the limiting beliefs you have about yourself.

No one can ever go beyond the self-image or self-concept he holds. It's impossible—beliefs determine your experience. If you can't see yourself doing it or being it, forget it. It won't happen. On the other hand, if you can hold on to the dream and clear out all the limiting beliefs that say you can't, it's yours!

With all the self-help information available today, why isn't everyone happy and why don't people always get what they want?

Why are so many people struggling to achieve something only to give up in frustration?

How many self-help or motivational workshops have you attended only to have the excitement wear off after a short period of time? What do you think is really believed by an individual who affirms fifty times a day, "I'm rich. I'm rich. I'm rich." You guessed it, he really believes that he is *not* rich.

He is also strengthening the thoughtform that is already keeping him from being rich. He'll soon see no results for his efforts and give up in frustration. His limiting belief could have to do with money, but most often it has to do with a personal belief, such as the belief that he does not deserve it or a related belief.

One of the lessons I had to learn the hard way when I began exploring belief systems back in 1988 was that experiences are determined by the sum total of your beliefs and your point of mental focus, your attention—not just the experience you selectively choose to create.

I decided that since I had all this profound knowledge of how the universe works, I would get up the next morning and simply create what I wanted. Well, it didn't work and, as you might guess, I generated a lot of frustration and anger for myself. I guess I had a transparent belief about how I learn things—the hard way.

As we've seen, beliefs can be empowering or limiting. Limiting beliefs negate or subtract from empowering beliefs and desires. What do you get when you add +2 and −2? You're right—zero! This is the part that didn't sink in for me. I was still trapped into believing that if I tried hard enough to believe in what I wanted, I didn't have to pay attention to my limitations. I didn't think that I had many anyway. Just ask me.

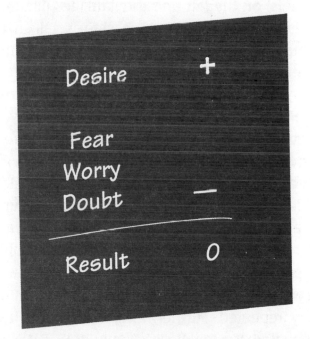

But there I was, using my old belief: "If I would just try harder, I could succeed." I soon learned that old beliefs continue to gain strength and become dominating. After I realized what was happening, I refocused my efforts to working on my liabilities—my limiting beliefs. Yes, I did find some—many. After a while it became a treat to find them. It meant that I was one step closer to being clear.

To use an analogy, refer to the balance sheet illustration. Here, as in traditional accounting, are two columns: the assets (empowering beliefs) on the left and the liabilities (limiting beliefs) on the right. Each side is tallied to obtain the "total assets" on the left and the "total liabilities" on the right.

At first glance we can see that the old limiting belief, "I NEVER GET WHAT I WANT," is very strong and powerful from years of having energy added to it. It will take forever to add enough "I am rich" beliefs to the left side of the balance sheet to try and overcome the strong limiting belief. First of all, the "I am rich," in this case, is not really a belief—it's only a statement. It's a wish or, at best, a hope. If it were a belief, it wouldn't have to be continually repeated. Furthermore, every time it is repeated, the real belief, "I NEVER GET WHAT I WANT," increases in strength to fulfill its original intent—to make sure that you don't.

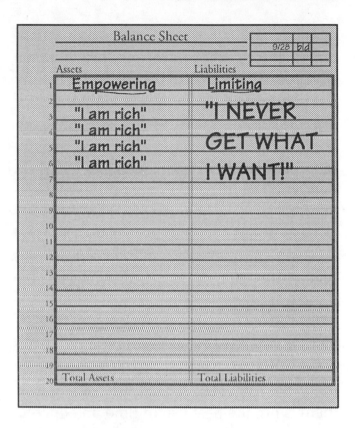

There are basically two limiting beliefs in action here:

1. "I never get what I want."
2. "I am not rich." (implied)

For any real improvement in this situation, the belief "I NEVER GET WHAT I WANT" must be eliminated.

There are numerous self-development books, tapes, and workshops available—all with good intent and of real benefit. In many cases, however, the benefit is temporary, for a good reason. Many techniques don't address the *cause* of your experiences. They try to implement new techniques that focus on overpowering or going around the old situation to create a new desired state. This approach requires ongoing diligence and constant effort which soon get tiresome and boring—the student usually gives up in frustration.

The main reason for limited success gets back to what we have been discussing—the cause—limiting beliefs. Old limiting beliefs must be removed. Trying to "overpower" them is not the best use of time and energy. What's required for *permanent* change in your experience is a shift from a focus on trying to overpower old beliefs with new ones to a focus on identifying and simply dissolving the old beliefs that no longer serve you. These limiting beliefs may have been appropriate when you were a child, but they hinder you as an adult.

It's like planting a flower garden. If you don't till the soil and pull out all the weeds before you plant, you'll end up with a field of weeds that has some flowers in it. An improvement, but not the desired result. Till the soil, remove the weeds, and then plant your seeds—in no time at all, you'll have a marvelous garden of your favorite flowers.

Another way to look at the same concept is to imagine trying to hit the bull's-eye on a

A New Approach

Dissolve old limiting beliefs.

target on the other side of a corn field. The corn stalks (limiting beliefs) resist and deflect the path of the arrow. Rather than try to force the arrow through the corn by pulling harder on the string, simply remove the corn stalks between you and the target. Now, with an accurate aim and normal pull, a bull's-eye is assured.

People spend significant effort and money looking for ways to get what they want—happiness, money, love, jobs—only to give up in frustration. The secret is to focus on dissolving barriers—those barriers are the limiting beliefs that are generating your life's frustrations and fears.

three

Get What You Want

Maintain a
Positive Environment

Let's take the knowledge that you have gained and make it work for you. The first thing to remember is that you will experience, for some period of time, the results of the

thoughtforms that you put into motion in the past. Recognize that this will occur, and begin to work from this moment forth to deliberately design the experiences you wish to have in the future.

What you need to do is create a positive environment for yourself while you explore prior choices that will continue to impact you. Begin creating a positive attitude about life by establishing your own version of "Everything happens for the best." I say "your version" because that's what is important. It's *your* beliefs that count—not mine.

Develop your version and strengthen the thoughtform when something occurs for you that might not initially seem favorable by reminding yourself that "everything happens for the best." It will take a little practice, but as you strengthen the thoughtform, you'll notice a difference in your emotional response. Adopt the philosophy that you can learn something from every experience.

To further enhance your environment, focus on the positive things around you. See the glass as half full rather than half empty. Be sure to focus your attention on what you want, not on what you don't want. If you desire more money, focus on how to obtain more—not on the fact that you don't have enough. Constantly keep in mind what you've learned about thoughtforms—you don't want to use your energy to strengthen limiting ones. Keep your attention focused on your desires and goals—strengthen those thoughtforms. Your overall intent should be to keep your energy positive. And you know what that means—the more you stay positive, the more you will attract positive experiences.

There are times, however, when you won't feel positive—that's only being human. I'm not encouraging you to deny or avoid unpleasant feelings or situations. Experiencing them is an important part of your growth process. I'm saying to experience them—but move on as quickly as possible. Develop your ability to emotionally rebound. As you remove limiting beliefs, doing so will become easier and easier.

I have a friend who was told by a counselor that to release his fears he needed to experience them. That may be true, but the experience need not last for years—experience and release can be done in a matter of minutes.

I used to have fun with my management team when something went wrong and we all felt discouraged. I'd say, "OK, we are going to sit here for five minutes and suck our thumbs and then forget it." We did and it worked. How long can you feel depressed looking at five other grown men sucking their thumbs!

Have Faith in Yourself

It's important also that you have the faith (belief) that you can make the changes in your life that you choose to make. If you have the belief that you can't help yourself change, stop right where you are because your disbelief will negate anything that you attempt to do. Remember, you can only change that for which you are willing to accept responsibility. So create your version of "I'm responsible for my own experiences and I can change my life for the better." You can do it! Just believe it. Believe in yourself.

I would encourage you not to establish expectations that everything in your life will miraculously change overnight. If it does, that's wonderful. Based on my experience, however, it may take some patience on your part. That may sound like a limiting statement, but I'd rather see you make incremental progress and stick with it, than go for the moon and quit in frustration. Your library of beliefs was built up over a number of years; it will take some research to access the inventory. The time to start the process of change, however, is right now.

Process is an important word. A process is something that happens over time. Change is a process. Unfortunately, most of us want change to be an event—instantaneous results. Life itself is a process—ever-changing, ever-unfolding. You're probably wondering how long your process of change will take. Realistically? Forever! Don't panic—you'll want to continue your own process of growth and change to expand and deepen your experiences—indefinitely. It becomes compelling. Personal growth is a lifelong process. So change what you want to change—at your own pace. You are experiencing your world. You call the shots.

Increase Your Self-Awareness

With the appropriate emotional environment established and the confidence that you can succeed, now you need to expand your awareness of yourself so you can begin to recognize your limiting beliefs.

Phrase Completion

One of the easiest ways of surfacing your beliefs is to do simple phrase completion exercises. The concept involves spontaneously completing the endings to certain phrases to allow the subconscious mind to bring forth uncensored information. When you get your logical, rational thought processes involved, you begin judging the information and the free-flow ceases. The Appendix contains exercises to help you surface some of your beliefs. To get a better feel for the concept, take a look at a few examples in the illustration.

Notice the number of limiting beliefs that surfaced. Do any of them look familiar?

Monitor Your Self-Talk

Monitoring your self-talk is an excellent way to start collecting data on what beliefs you hold. Self-talk is the constant mental and/or verbal conversation that goes on as you are going about your day. It's talking to yourself. For me it's usually mental. I am happy to say that since I started removing limiting thought-forms ten years ago, much of my critical self-talk has vanished. I can now find time to just experience the moment. You can do the same.

What usually happens when you're involved in self-talk is that you are not present mentally to experience the "now" that we discussed earlier. Self-talk has you either chewing over something that has already happened or agonizing over something that you're afraid will happen. Most of this self-talk is very limiting, about something you did or didn't do or about what someone else did or didn't do. Generally, it is nonproductive and judgmental. On the other hand, if you spend your day telling yourself how wonderful you are, that's great.

You can learn a lot about your limiting beliefs by being an observer of your self-talk. Make believe you are a miniature private investigator, and sit on your shoulder and take notes. What's this person focused on? Listen to your own beliefs. Write them down. How many of them are self-critical? Self criticism is very limiting. Learn to enjoy catching yourself in the act. "Aha, gotcha again."

Another approach to self-talk would be to ask a committed listener such as your spouse, a significant other, or a trusted friend to assist you by writing down what they hear you say, especially when you are upset. Just be sure you are ready for it—no denial, no being defensive, and please don't shoot the messenger! Just note the beliefs that they recorded and decide what you want to do with them. Are some of them limiting you?

Notice Your Reflections

Another technique to increase your awareness is to monitor your reflections in the universal mirror. Recall from the discussion on mirroring that the events, circumstances, and people that show up in your life are there to mirror back to you what you're projecting into the universe. To illustrate what I mean by events reflecting back to you, I'll share a personal experience with you.

One of my idiosyncrasies is orderliness. Everything must be in its place and things must be kept clean and tidy at all times. Normally this trait is an asset but taken to extreme it becomes a liability. One of the things that irritates me is loose hair—cat hair, dog hair, human hair, it doesn't matter. For years, I've had very little; fortunately my former mate liked bald heads. Her hair was beautiful—chestnut brown and very long.

About two years ago, I was sitting in the bathroom getting very irritated about the long brown hair that I noticed littering the floor. My mental conversation was very judgmental about her not cleaning up after herself. As I sat there getting more irritated, I had a jolting thought: "Oh, my god, what if there was no hair at all?"

In that moment, something shifted and the hair on the floor became a reminder to me of how lucky I was that she was in my life. It brought tears of joy to my eyes. Does your spouse leave the top off of the toothpaste, or put the toilet paper on the roll backwards? Great! Now you have a reminder, too, of how lucky you are.

If you have not already started a list of reflections that bother you, please start one and continue to update it as situations arise. As you encounter situations that "hook" you, ask yourself, "What do I believe is happening here?" Make a note of your answer. In the Appendix, I'll give you some hints on how to process this information.

Keep in mind, also, what I said about reflections from other people. A judgment that you assign to someone else is a judgment you are projecting. You are essentially assigning the judgment to yourself. For example, if you notice someone else's behavior and label that person "a know-it-all," what does that say about you? My guess is that it reflects your insecurity about "not knowing it all."

When you judge, there is an aspect of your personality that you haven't accepted. It's probably related to not feeling smart enough or maybe feeling inadequate about not having a degree or some acceptable (to you) level of credentials or training. If you felt good about yourself, another person's behavior wouldn't "hook" you.

That's the mirror—it reflects back to you information to learn more about yourself. When you notice that you are judging someone, ask yourself, "If this is what I believe about that person, what does that say about me?" Remember what I said earlier about not judging yourself for judging others. It will take some time to shift your judgments—if you choose to do so. In the meantime, acknowledge yourself for having the guts to work on it.

Remove Limiting Thoughtforms

To remove limiting thoughtforms, you utilize the same method that you used when you acquired them. You used *choice*. To remove them, you also use choice. You just choose to do so. This may sound too simple, but that's how it works. There are several copyrighted techniques that detail processes for removing unwanted thoughtforms, but the basic element of removal is the aspect of choice.

The actual removal step is simple, but the challenge for most people is getting to that point—mentally. Can you imagine "fire walking" by yourself if you read in a book that all you had to do was concentrate on the belief that you are walking on wet, moist, velvety grass? I don't think you would take off your shoes until you had some coaching. The techniques for removing thoughtforms are of the same nature. Confidence must be built with smaller experiences of success before most people will believe that they can do it. We all have existing beliefs about what can and cannot be done. They must be dealt with first. Also, when you remove a limiting thought-form it's a good idea to replace it with an empowering one. Here's a simple example.

Let's say that you uncovered the limiting belief "Nothing ever works for me." First, put

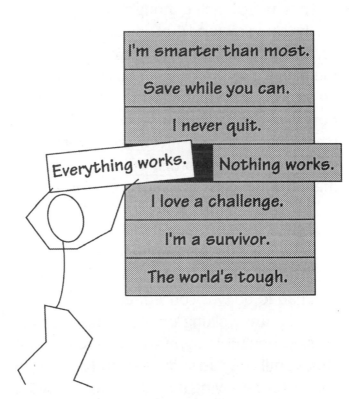

your full concentration on that belief and then say to yourself slowly and deliberately, either mentally or verbally, "I have the belief 'Nothing works for me,' and I choose to remove it from my belief system because it limits me." That's all it takes. To replace it, just choose a new one. "I choose to replace it with 'Everything that I do works out for my best interest.'"

If you will recall the grapevine structure of thoughtforms, you will notice that each time

Thoughtform Structure

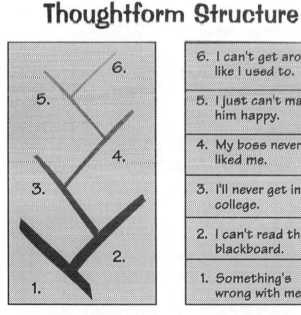

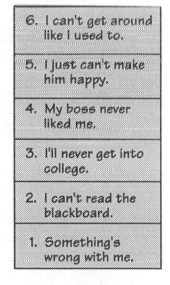

6. I can't get around like I used to.

5. I just can't make him happy.

4. My boss never liked me.

3. I'll never get into college.

2. I can't read the blackboard.

1. Something's wrong with me.

Grapevine
Model

List
Model

you remove a thoughtform, you're working your way down the vine until you come to the root cause thoughtform.

Another way to look at it would be to convert the branches of each stem into a list with the "root" thoughtform at the bottom of the list as in the figure. The similar thought-forms generated subsequently get layered on top of the previously created one. The most recently generated one would therefore be at the top of the list (the tip of the branch).

For those with the confidence to forge ahead at removing limiting thoughtforms, here is the secret that I finally learned. Use the removing-limiting-thoughtforms technique on your doubts as well. Doubt is what used to stop me. "Did it work? Am I doing it right? It doesn't seem to be working today. Some-thing's wrong. I need more experience. I need help." Every thought of this nature will hinder your progress because, as you've learned, thoughtforms will act to fulfill themselves. When you think, "Something's wrong," guess what you've just created. So, when a doubt shows up, just use the technique to get rid of it and keep going.

Here's Another Example

Let's say you want to remove the limiting belief "Nobody cares about what I have to say." As you begin, you have the thought, "I'm not sure I know how to do this right." That now becomes the limiting belief that you work on. Start with "I have the belief 'I am not sure I know how to do this right' and I choose to remove it from my belief system because it limits me."

Then you have the thought, "I'm not sure that worked." Do the same thing. "I have the belief 'I'm not sure that worked' and I choose to remove it from my belief system because it limits me."

Then go to the original limiting belief, "Nobody cares about what I have to say." If another doubt shows up before you removed the original limiting belief, treat it the same way—remove it. Initially, don't be surprised if a number of these pesky doubts show up. Just cheer for yourself that you found another one and remove it. Keep going—it will get easier and easier.

Go Exploring

It is my hope that the information you have just read will entice you into further exploration of how your beliefs impact your life's experience. The Appendix contains some simple exercises to help you increase your awareness.

My wish is for every person on the planet—especially our young people—to have some insight into the fundamentals of thought and the power that we all have at our disposal to design our lives deliberately. We all have the innate ability to create anything that we can imagine. The holographic universe is energetically structured to turn every desire into reality if that desire is not impaired by a previously created conflicting belief. Only your own beliefs hold you back.

I'd like to leave you with one more insight—the thoughtform that will attract the most positive circumstances into your life is "I love myself."

Appendix

I suggest that you do the exercises in the Appendix in a notebook so you can retain your work for future reference. It will give you an excellent benchmark from which to witness your progress.

Phrase Completion

In a notebook write as many endings as you can, as quickly as you can, for the "I am _____" phrases in each category. Let your mind free-flow. Your answers don't have to be logical or make sense.

I am _____.
   (Physical Characteristics)

I am _____.
   (Emotional)

I am _____.
   (Mental)

I am _____.
   (Social)

I am _____.
   (Career)

I am _____.
(*Relationships*)

I am _____.
(*Love*)

I am _____.
(*Family*)

Similarly, complete as many phrases as you can for the following:

_____ makes me feel happy.

_____ makes me feel sad.

_____ makes me feel angry.

_____ makes me feel guilty.

Men are _____.

Women are _____.

Babies are _____.

Puppies are _____.

Money is _____.

People are _____.

Sex is _____.

Life is _____.

Love is _____.

I am a _____ person.

I can _____.

I can't _____.

I should _____.

I shouldn't _____.

It's wrong to _____.

I am too _____.

I _____ myself.

After you have completed the exercise, make a note beside each of your responses for empowering beliefs (E) and for limiting beliefs (L). Quite revealing, isn't it? How many of these limiting beliefs would you like to eliminate?

Reflections

To begin the process, select an item from your list of things that bother you—one that has a great deal of emotional charge attached to it. Something that really disturbs you. Write in your notebook your answers to the following questions for the item you selected.

1. When you noticed unpleasant feelings, what did you believe was happening?

2. Can you think of another belief that may also be valid in this situation?

3. How many other beliefs can you think of?

4. Seeing that there are other beliefs (perspectives), can you now let go of

the original belief that you had,
knowing that it's only one perspective of many?

Example

Here's an illustration. Situation: "Every time
someone goes into my boss's office and
closes the door, I feel uneasy."

1. When you noticed unpleasant feelings, what did you believe was happening?

   "I felt as though they were talking
   about me."

2. Can you think of another belief that
   may also be valid in this situation?

   "They may have been talking about
   someone else."

3. How many other beliefs can you
   think of?

   "They may not have been talking
   about anyone else. They may have

been discussing his or her perform-
ance. They may have been working
out a schedule. He or she may have
just had a question about a work
assignment."

4. Seeing that there are other beliefs
(perspectives), can you now let go of
the original belief that you had,
knowing that it's only one perspective of many?

"Gosh, how silly of me to assume that
just because the door is closed, they
are talking about me. There are
many things they could have been
discussing. You know, it reminds me
of when I was young. When my dad
would come home from work, he
and my mother would talk in their
bedroom behind closed doors while
he was changing his clothes. If she
reported that I had misbehaved during the day, he would whip me. I
guess when people are talking behind closed doors at the office, it
seems the same. From now on, I sure
won't assume that people are talking

about me when their door is closed—that's ridiculous."

Bringing the situation to this new level of awareness will often resolve the issue.

Summary Points
for Reflection

Thoughts exist as thoughtforms.

Thoughts generate feelings.

Thoughtforms exist to fulfill their intent.

Thoughtforms attract similar thoughtforms.

Thoughts that I accept as true become
my beliefs.

Beliefs are specialized thoughtforms.

Beliefs determine my experiences.

The sum of my beliefs makes up my
individual belief system.

My individual belief system generates my energetic signature.

My energetic signature attracts my life's circumstances.

Beliefs are empowering or limiting.

Limiting beliefs inhibit the expression of my true self.

What I focus my attention on expands in my life.

Attention strengthens thoughtforms.

I keep my attention focused on my goals.

Self-responsibility creates inner power.

My external events (experiences) are determined by my internal events (beliefs).

The universe mirrors my beliefs back to me.

Judgments, fear, worry, and doubt are all tied to limiting beliefs.

It's important to stay positive to attract positive circumstances.

Everything happens for the best.

Experiencing is feeling.

I can only experience in the present moment—now.

I experience my beliefs about the past—not the past itself.

Limiting beliefs negate my desires.

Old limiting beliefs become stronger when challenged.

Beliefs are added and removed by choice.

Stay positive.

Believe in myself.

Increase my self-awareness.

Remove the limiting thoughtforms that I choose to remove.

Create what I want.

Love myself.

The accumulation of all of my individual beliefs makes up my belief system.

Belief precedes experience.

My energetic signature attracts my life's circumstances.

Everyone has his own truth.

What I focus on expands in my life.

Judgments are tied to beliefs.

Dissolve old limiting beliefs.

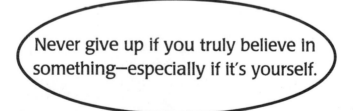

Never give up if you truly believe in something—especially if it's yourself.

About the Author

Bruce has over twenty-five years of experience as a corporate executive and business consultant focused on organizational and individual transformation. He is recognized as an inspirational leader who creates transformation based on his philosophy, "Lead the People—Manage the Business!" This philosophy embraces the value of leading from the heart to create an environment that fosters integrity and open, honest relationships to facilitate the mutual achievement of both individual and corporate goals.

He holds B.S. and M.S. degrees in Electrical Engineering from Penn State University and Virginia Polytechnic Institute. He enjoys flying and is an instrument-rated private pilot. Bruce is dedicated to helping individuals achieve their full potential through the realization that their beliefs create their life experiences.

If you are interested in exploring the concept "Beliefs determine your experience" at a deeper level, there are courses scheduled around the country. For dates and locations, write to the author in care of Hampton Roads Publishing.

Hampton Roads Publishing Company

. . .for the evolving human spirit

Hampton Roads Publishing Company
publishes and distributes books on a variety of subjects,
including metaphysics, health, complementary medicine,
visionary fiction, and other related subjects.

To order or receive a copy of our latest catalog, call toll-free,
(800) 766-8009, or send your name and address to:

Hampton Roads Publishing Company, Inc.
134 Burgess Lane
Charlottesville, VA 22902